Mel Bay Presents Stefan Grossman's Guitar Workshop

The Mu

Grateful Dead®

arranged for fingerstyle guitar

Taught by Fred Sokolow

CONTENTS

GUITAR WORKSHOP

Visit us on the Web at www.melbay.com — E-mail us at email@melbay.com

1 2 3 4 5 6 7 8 9 0

CHORDS

Whenever up-the-neck or unusual chords are used in the arrangements that follow, they are pictured (with grids) in the tablature. Otherwise, use these familiar, first-position chords:

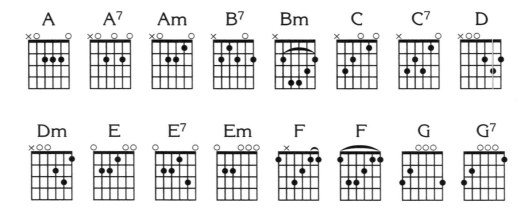

HOW TO READ SONG ROADMAPS

This book uses the standard notation found in most songbooks, including repeat signs, codas and so on. Here are some tips on reading these signals:

REPEAT SIGNS

A double bar line with the heavy line on the left and dots on the right hand side ‖ means you're beginning a section of the tune that will be repeated. When you see another double bar line with the heavy line on the right and dots pointing left ‖ go back to the repeat sign that points the other way and repeat that section once. Sometimes there's a notation telling you to repeat it more than once, such as *repeat four times*, or *4x*.

I lit out— from Re-no, I was chased by twen-ty hounds.
Did-n't get— to sleep that night 'til morn-ing rolled a-round.

FIRST AND SECOND ENDINGS

Some repeated sections have alternate endings. To play the measure below, play the first six bars and play the *first ending* (bars 7 and 8). Then repeat bars 1–6 and play the *second ending* (bars 9 and 10).

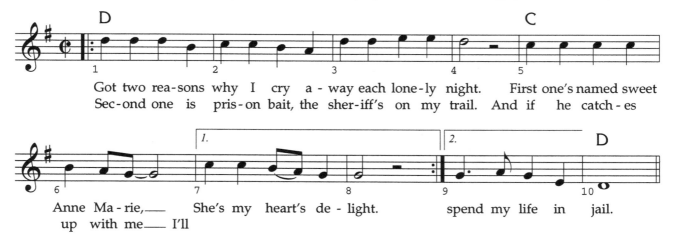

Got two rea-sons why I cry a-way each lone-ly night. First one's named sweet
Sec-ond one is pris-on bait, the sher-iff's on my trail. And if he catch-es

Anne Ma-rie,— She's my heart's de-light. spend my life in jail.
up with me— I'll

D.C. AL CODA

The notation "D.C. al Coda," written above the music notation, usually toward the end of a tune, tells you to start over from the beginning and keep playing until you see a "to Coda" notation next to a Coda sign ⊕. At that point, skip to the Coda, an ending clearly marked as "Coda" with that same sign, and play it through to the end. See an example below, under "EXAMPLES."

D.S. AL CODA

This is the same as above, with one difference: when you see "D.S. al Coda," instead of going back to the beginning, you go back to the D.S. sign ‰ and start over from that point. As above, when you reach the "to Coda" indication, skip ahead to the Coda.

EXAMPLES

Friend of the Devil (Fingerpicking Arrangement)
- Play the 4-bar Intro/Verse. The repeat signs at the beginning and end of the Verse tell you to play those four bars twice.
- The Chorus begins with four bars enclosed by repeat signs, so play those four bars twice. Notice the *Last time to Coda* indication…but move on.
- Play the next four bars, which are an instrumental tag to the Bridge.
- Play the Bridge. The eighth bar of the Bridge is a 1st ending. After playing it, repeat the Bridge, but this time skip the 1st ending and play the 2nd ending instead.
- Continue on, and after a few bars, you come to the Solo.
- At the end of the Solo, the D.C. indication tells you to start over again at the very beginning of the tune. Don't forget to repeat the sections you repeated the first time.
- When you get to the *Last time to Coda* indication, jump ahead to the Coda (at the very end of the tune), and play that last bar.

Alabama Getaway (Fingerpicking Arrangement)
- The 2-bar Intro is enclosed by repeat signs, so play it twice.
- So is the 8-bar Verse, so play it twice.
- Play the 8-bar Chorus. Notice the *To Coda* sign at the 7th bar.
- Continue with the 8-bar Solo, which is in repeat signs. Play it twice.
- The second time around the Solo, the *D.S. al Coda* tells you to go back to the D.S. sign ‰, which is at the beginning of the Verse, and start over from that point. Take the same repeats as before.
- When you get to the 7th bar of the Chorus, skip ahead to the Coda, and play the final two bars of the arrangement.

FRED SOKOLOW HAS OTHER INSTRUCTIONAL BOOKS, TAPES, VIDEOS
& CDs. FOR A FREE CATALOG, WRITE TO

SOKOLOW MUSIC
PO BOX 491264
LOS ANGELES CA 90049

OR LOG ON TO http://members.aol.com/sokolowmus/

FRIEND OF THE DEVIL

by Garcia, Hunter & Dawson   Copyright © 1970 Ice Nine Publishing Company, Inc.

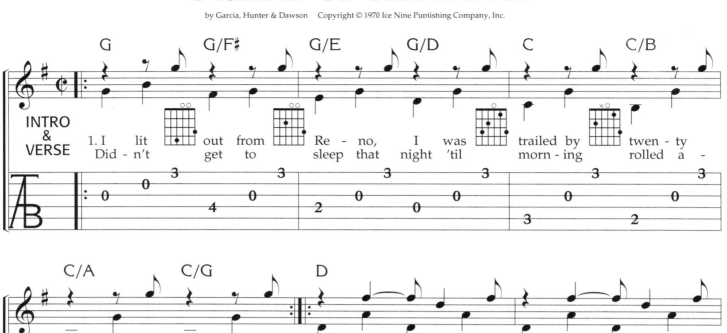

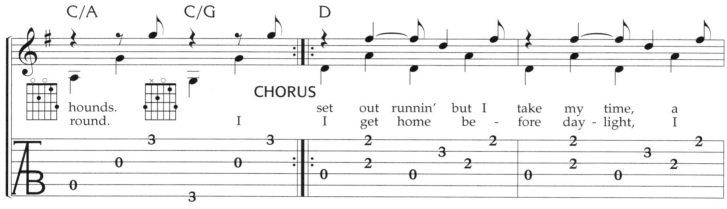

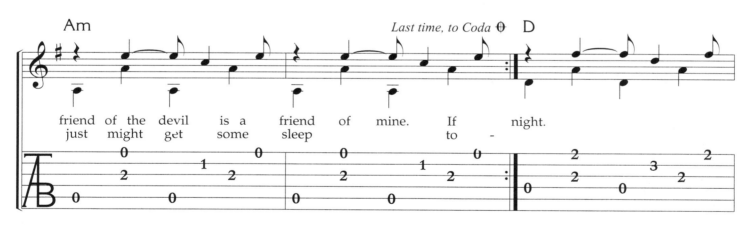

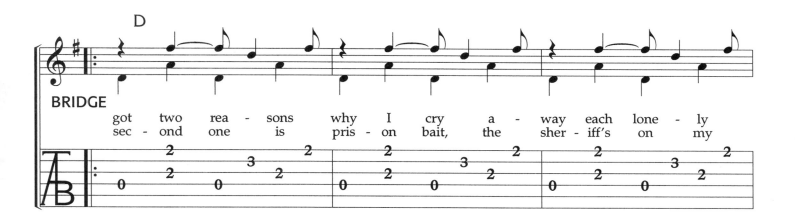

BRIDGE

got two rea - sons why I cry a - way each lone - ly
sec - ond one is why pris - on bait, the sher - iff's on my

night.   The   first one's named Sweet Ann - Ma - rie,
trail, and if he catch - es up with me, I'll

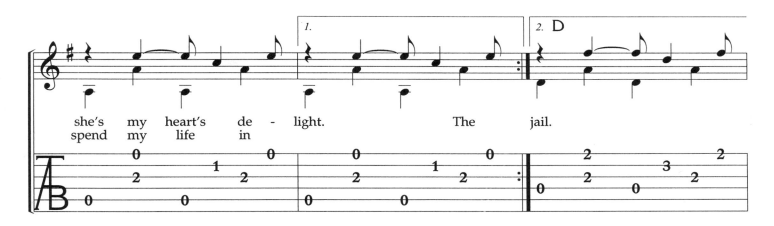

she's my heart's de - light.   The   jail.
spend my life in

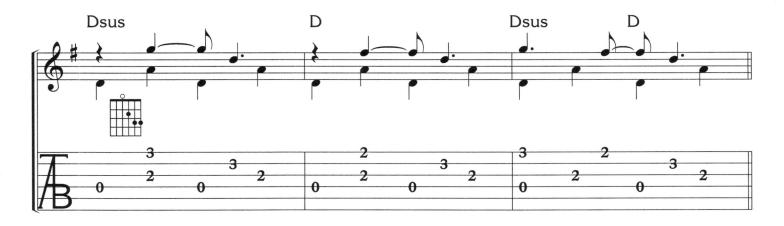

5

FRIEND OF THE DEVIL
LEAD SHEET

by Garcia, Hunter & Dawson   Copyright © 1970 Ice Nine Publishing Company, Inc.

FRIEND OF THE DEVIL

1. I lit out from Reno, I was trailed by twenty hounds.
   Didn't get to sleep that night 'til morning came around.

   Chorus:
   I set out runnin' but I take my time, a friend of the devil is a friend of mine.
   If I get home before daylight, just might get some sleep tonight.

2. Ran into the devil, babe, he loaned me twenty bills.
   I spent the night in Utah in a cave up in the hills.   *(chorus)*

3. I ran down to the levee but the devil caught me there.
   He took my twenty dollar bill and vanished in the air.   *(chorus)*

   Bridge:
   Got two reasons why I cry away each lonely night.
   First one's named sweet Ann-Marie, she's my heart's delight.
   Second one is prison bait, the sheriff's on my trail,
   And if he catches up with me I'll spend my life in jail.

4. Got a wife in Chino, babe, one in Cherokee.
   First one say she's got my child but it don't look like me.   *(chorus)*

Deal

by Garcia & Hunter   Copyright © 1971 Ice Nine Publishing Company, Inc.

INTRO

VERSE Since you've poured the

wine for me   and tightened up our shoes,   I hate to see you

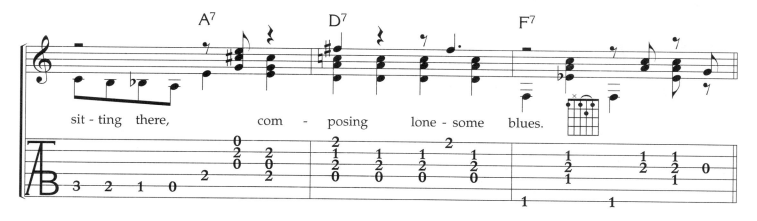

sit - ting there,   com - posing lone - some blues.

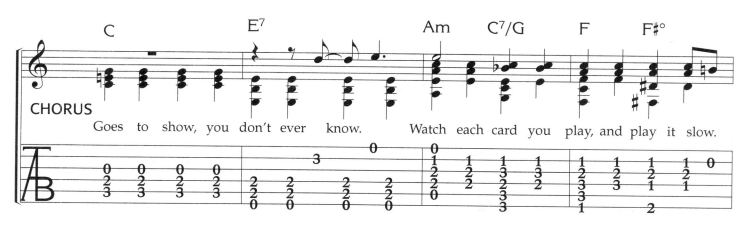

CHORUS Goes to show, you don't ever know.   Watch each card you play, and play it slow.

Don't you let that deal go down. hmm.
Wait un - til that deal comes 'round, mm -

SOLO

DEAL

LEAD SHEET

by Garcia & Hunter   Copyright © 1971 Ice Nine Publishing Company, Inc.

1. Since it costs a lot to win and even more to lose,
   You and me bound to spend some time wond'ring what to choose.

   Chorus:
   Goes to show, you don't ever know.
   Watch each card you play and play it slow.
   Wait until that deal comes round.
   Don'cha let that deal go down, no, no.

2. I've been gamblin' hereabouts for ten good solid years.
   If I told you 'bout all that went down, it might burn off both your ears.
   (chorus)

3. Since you poured the wine for me and tightened up our shoes,
   I hate to see you sitting there composing lonesome blues.
   (chorus)

RIPPLE

by Garcia & Hunter   Copyright © 1971 Ice Nine Publishing Company, Inc.

SOLO (VERSE)

CHORUS

VERSE

There is a road,   no sim - ple high - way,

between   the dawn   and the

dark   of   night.   And if you   go

no - one   will   follow.

That   path   is   for   your   steps a -

lone.   CHORUS   Ripple   in   still

water,   when there is no pebble

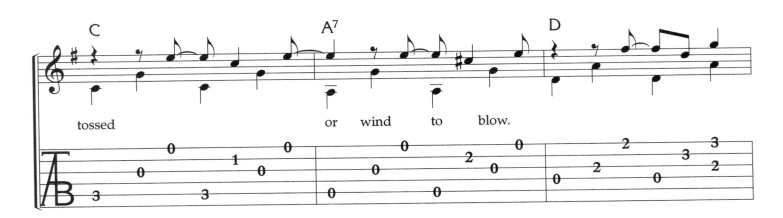

tossed   or   wind   to   blow.

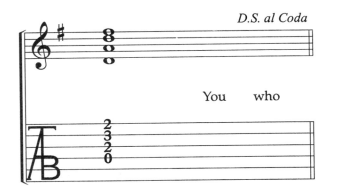

D.S. al Coda

You   who

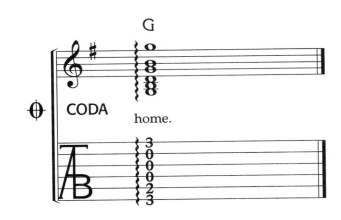

CODA   home.

Ripple Lead Sheet

by Garcia & Hunter   Copyright © 1971 Ice Nine Publishing Company, Inc.

1. If my words did glow with the gold of sunshine
   and my tunes were played on the harp unstrung,
   Would you hear my voice come through the music,
   would you hold it near as if it were your own?

2. It's a hand me down, the thoughts are broken.
   Perhaps they're better left unsung.
   I don't know, don't really care.
   Let there be songs to fill the air.

   Chorus:
   Ripple in still water,
      when there is no pebble tossed,
      nor wind to blow.

3. Reach out your hand if your cup be empty.
   If your cup is full, may it be again.
   Let it be known there is a fountain
   that was not made by the hands of man.

4. There is a road, no simple highway,
   between the dawn and the dark of night.
   And if you go, no one may follow,
   that path is for your steps alone. *(chorus)*

5. You who choose to lead must follow,
   but if you fall, you fall alone.
   If you should stand, then who's to guide you?
   If I knew the way, I would take you home.

Alabama Getaway

by Garcia & Hunter   Copyright © 1982 Ice Nine Publishing Company, Inc.

INTRO

VERSE
Thirty - two teeth in a
reason the poor girls

jawbone,
love him, he'll Alabama promise them tryin' for any - none. thing. Be -

fore I have to hit him,   I hope he's got the sense to run.
Why they all be - lieve him, he wears a big diamond ring.

CHORUS
The Al - a - bam - a get - a - way,   get - a - way,

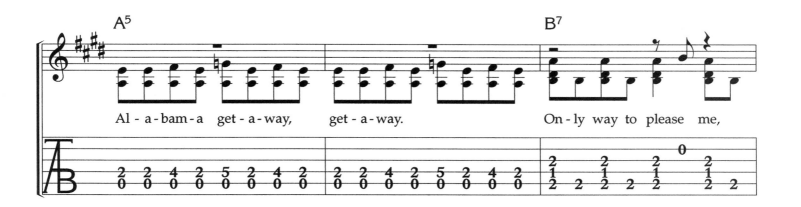

Al - a - bam - a get - a - way, get - a - way. On - ly way to please me,

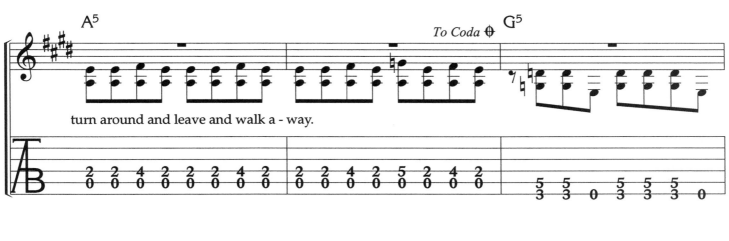

turn around and leave and walk a - way.

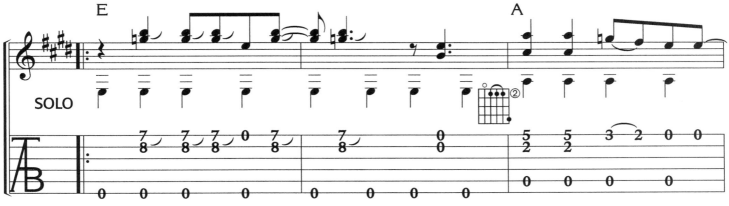

SOLO

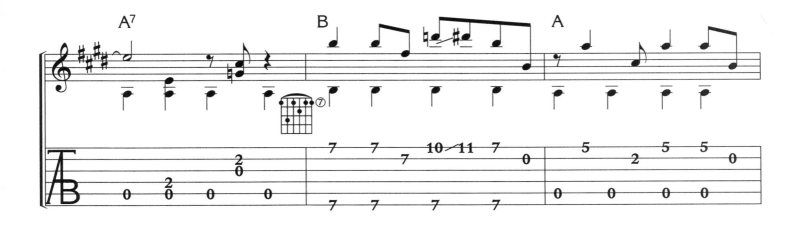

19

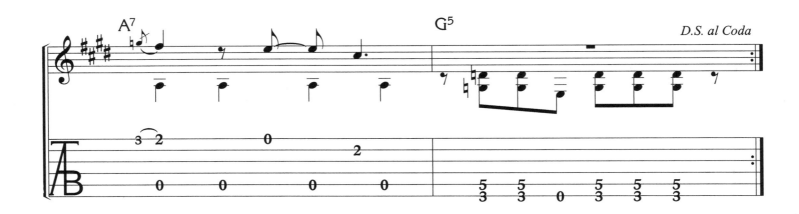

D.S. al Coda

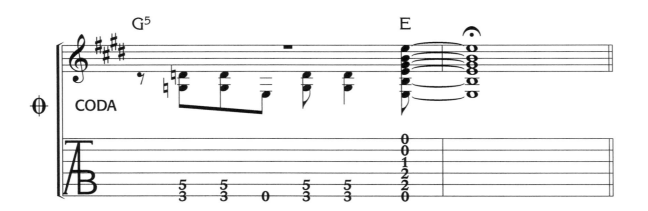

CODA

ALABAMA GETAWAY

LEAD SHEET

by Garcia & Hunter   Copyright © 1982 Ice Nine Publishing Company, Inc.

1. Thirty-two teeth in a jawbone, Alabama tryin' for none.
   Before I have to hit him, I hope he's got the sense to run.

2. Reason the poor girls love him, promise them anything.
   Why they all believe him, he wears a big diamond ring.

   Chorus:
   Alabama getaway, getaway, Alabama getaway, getaway.
   Only way to please me, turn around and leave and walk away.
   (Just get up and leave and walk away.)

3. Major-Domo Billy Bojangles, sit down and have a drink with me.
   What's this about Alabama, it keeps a-comin' back to me?

4. I heard your plea in the court house, witness box began to rock and rise.
   Forty-nine sister states all had Alabama in their eyes.   *(chorus)*

Dire Wolf

by Garcia & Hunter Copyright © 1970 Ice Nine Publishing Company, Inc.

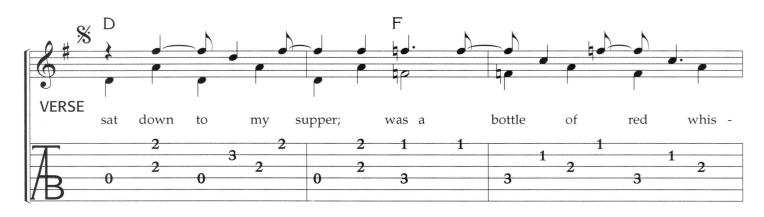

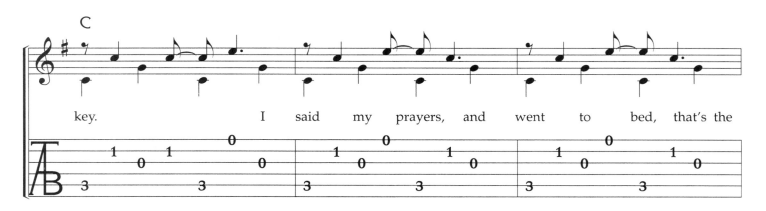

I beg of you, don't murder me.

Please   don't murder me.   When

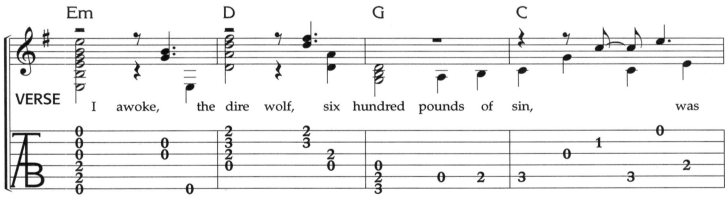

VERSE   I awoke,   the dire wolf,   six hundred pounds of sin,   was

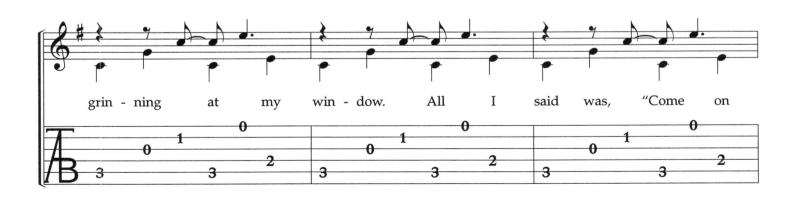

grin - ning   at   my   win - dow.   All   I   said was, "Come on

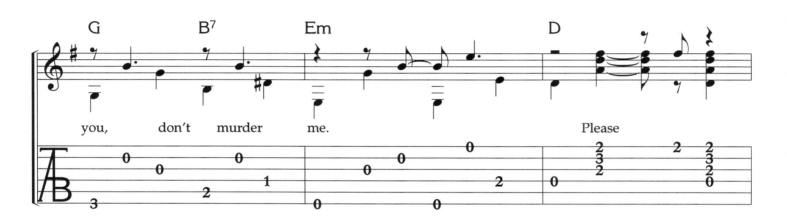

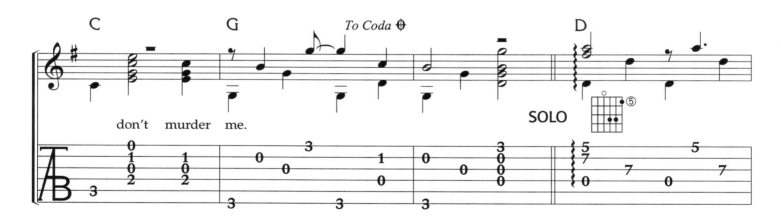

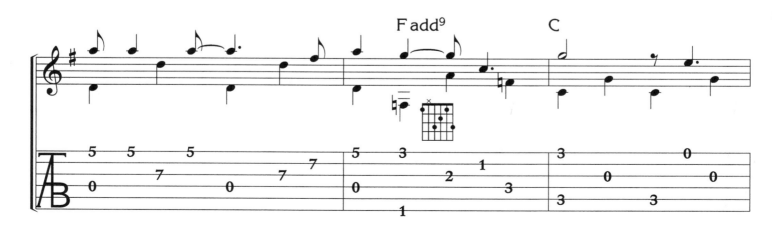

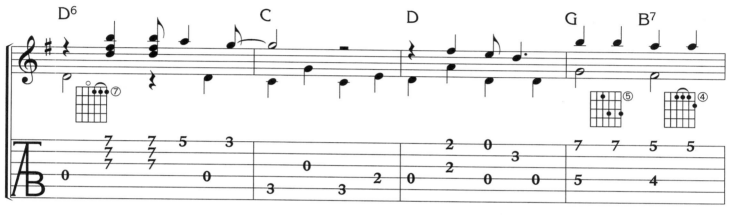

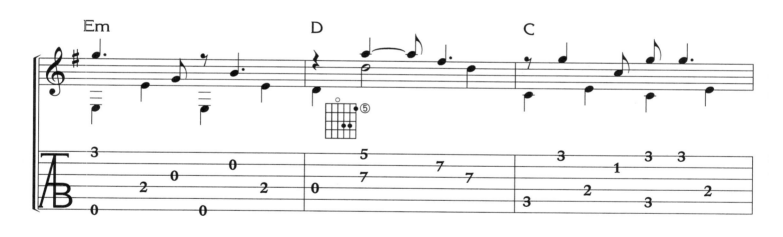

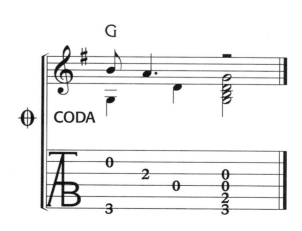

Dire Wolf
Lead Sheet

by Garcia & Hunter   Copyright © 1970 Ice Nine Publishing Company, Inc.

1. In the timbers of Fennario, the wolves are runnin' 'round.
   The winter was so hard and cold, froze ten feet 'neath the ground.

   Chorus:
   Don't murder me, I beg of you,
   Don't murder me, please don't murder me.

2. I sat down to my supper, 'twas a bottle of red whiskey.
   I said my prayers, went to bed, that's the last they saw of me.
   (chorus)

3. When I awoke, the dire wolf, six hundred pounds of sin,
   Was grinning at my window. All I said was, "Come on in."
   (chorus)

4. The wolf came in, I got my cards, we sat down for a game.
   I cut my deck to the queen of hearts, but the cards were all the same.
   (chorus)

5. In the backwash of Fennario, the black and bloody mire,
   The dire wolf collects his due while the boys sing 'round the fire.
   (chorus)
   (chorus)

27

Uncle John's Band

by Garcia & Hunter Copyright © 1970 Ice Nine Publishing Company, Inc.

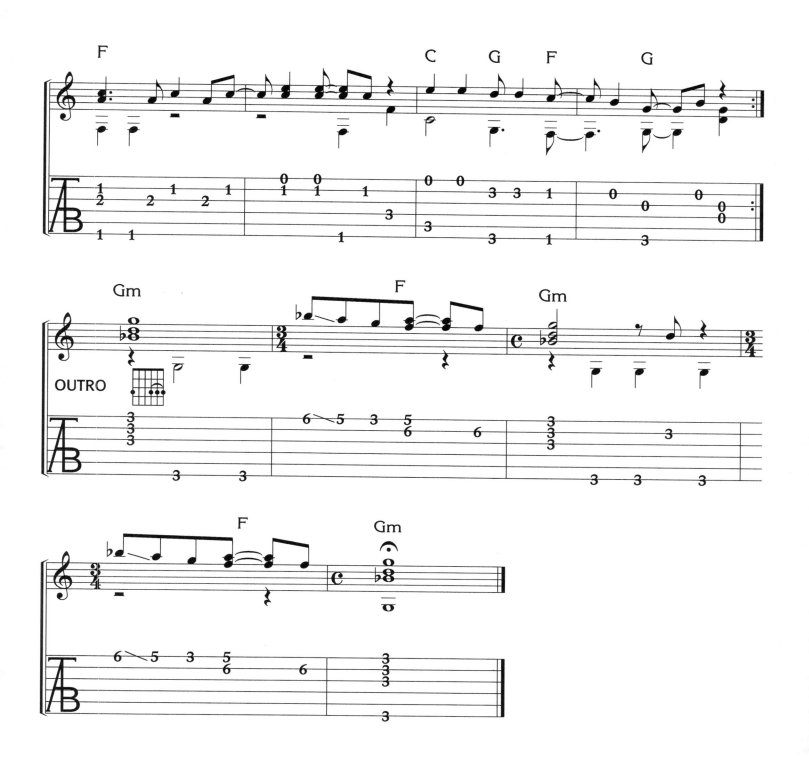

UNCLE JOHN'S BAND

by Garcia & Hunter Copyright © 1970 Ice Nine Publishing Company, Inc.

1. Well, the first days are the hardest days. Don't you worry anymore.
   'Cause when life looks like Easy Street there is danger at your door.
   Think this through with me, let me know your mind.
   What I want to know is, are you kind?

2. It's a buckdancer's choice, my friend, better take my advice.
   You know all the rules by now and the fire from the ice.
   Will you come with me? Won't you come with me?
   Wo, I want to know, will you come with me?

   Chorus:
   God damn, well I declare, have you seen the like?
   Their walls are built with cannonballs, their motto is
      "Don't tread on me."
   Come hear Uncle John's band playing to the tide.
   Come with me or go alone, he's come to take his children home.

3. It's the same story the crow told me, it's the only one he knows.
   Like the morning sun you come and like the wind you go.
   Ain't no time to hate, barely time to wait.
   What I want to know, where does the time go?

4. I lived in a silver mine and I call it Beggar's Tomb.
   I got me a violin and I beg you call the tune.
   Anybody's choice, I can hear your voice.
   What I want to know is, how does the song go?

   Chorus:
   Come hear Uncle John's band by the riverside.
   Got some things to talk about here beside the rising tide.
   Come hear Uncle John's band playing to the tide.
   Come with me or go alone, he's come to take his children home.

TOUCH OF GREY

by Garcia & Hunter Copyright © 1984 Ice Nine Publishing Company, Inc.

35

Touch of Grey

Lead Sheet

by Garcia & Hunter Copyright © 1984 Ice Nine Publishing Company, Inc.

1. It must be getting early, clocks are running late.
   Paint-by-numbers morning sky looks so phony.
   Dawn is breaking everywhere. Light a candle, curse the glare.
   Draw the curtains, I don't care 'cause it's all right.

   Chorus:
   I will get by, I will get by, I will get by, I will survive.

2. I see you've got your fist out. Say your piece and get out.
   Yes I got the gist of it, but it's alright.
   Sorry that you feel that way. The only thing there is to say:
   Every silver lining's got a touch of grey.
   (chorus)

   Bridge:
   It's a lesson to me, the Abels and the Bakers and the Cees.
   The ABCs we all must face, tryin' to keep a little grace.

3. I know the rent is in arrears, the dog has not been fed in years.
   It's even worse than it appears but it's alright.
   Cows are giving kerosene. The kid can't read at seventeen.
   The words he knows are all obscene but it's alright.
   (chorus)

   Bridge:
   It's a lesson to me, the Deltas and the east and the freeze.
   The ABCs we all think of, tryin' to keep a little love.

3. The shoe is on the hand it fits, there's really nothing much to it.
   Whistle through your teeth and spit 'cause it's all right.
   Oh well, a touch of grey kinda suits you, anyway.
   That was all I had to say, but it's alright.
   (chorus)

Sugar Magnolia

by Garcia & Hunter   Copyright © 1970 Ice Nine Publishing Company, Inc.

Come on, baby, come along with me.

CHORUS

She's got every- - - thing de-lightful,
Breeze in the pines and the sun and bright moonlight,

1. she's got every-thing I need.

2. lazing in the sunshine, yes in-

deed.

D.S. al Coda

41

CODA
sometimes when the night is dyin', I take me out and I wander 'round.

I wander 'round.

Sunshine daydream, walkin' in the tall trees,
goin' where the wind blows, bloomin' like a red rose.

(see lead sheet for additional lyrics)

ENDING

Sugar Magnolia — Solo

by Garcia & Hunter   Copyright © 1970 Ice Nine Publishing Company, Inc.

Sugar Magnolia

Lead Sheet

by Garcia & Hunter   Copyright © 1970 Ice Nine Publishing Company, Inc.

To Chorus, then v.5

5. Some - times— when the cuck - oo's cry - in', and the moon— is half - way down,— some - times— when the night is dy - in', I take me out— and I wan - der 'round.———— I wan - der 'round.—— Sun - shine— day - dream,— walk-in' in the tall trees.—

SUGAR MAGNOLIA

1. Sugar Magnolia, blossoms bloomin', head's all empty and I don't care.
   Saw my baby down by the river, knew she'd have to come up soon for air.

2. Sweet blossom, come on under the willow,
   we can have high times if you'll abide.
   We can discover the wonders of nature,
   wading in the rushes down by the riverside.

   Chorus:
   She's got everything delightful, She's got everything I need.
   Takes the wheel when I'm seein' double, pays my ticket when I speed.

3. She comes skimming through rays of violet. She can wade in a drop of dew.
   She don't come and I don't follow, waits backstage while I sing to you.

   Chorus:
   She's got everything delightful, She's got everything I need.
   Breeze in the pines and the sun and bright moonlight,
   lazing in the sunshine, yes indeed.

4. She can dance a Cajun rhythm, jump like a Willys in four-wheel drive.
   She's a summer love in the spring, fall and winter.
   She can make happy any man alive.

   Interlude:
   Sugar Magnolia, ringin' that bluebell, caught up in sunlight.
   Come on out singin'. I'll walk you in the sunshine.
   Come on, honey, come along with me.

5. Sometimes when the cuckoo's cryin', when the moon is halfway down,
   Sometimes when the night is dyin', I take me out and I wander 'round.
   I wander 'round.

   Coda:
   Sunshine daydream, walkin' in the tall trees,
   Goin' where the wind goes, blooming like a red rose.
   Breathin' more freely, ride out singin',
   I'll walk you in the morning sunshine.
   Sunshine daydream, sunshine daydream, walkin' in the sunshine.

TRUCKIN'

by Garcia, Hunter, Weir & Lesh   Copyright © 1971 Ice Nine Publishing Company, Inc.

if you don't lay 'em down, down."

BRIDGE
Sometimes the light's all shinin' on me,

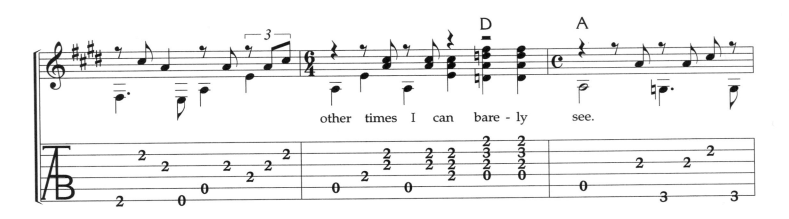

other times I can bare-ly see.

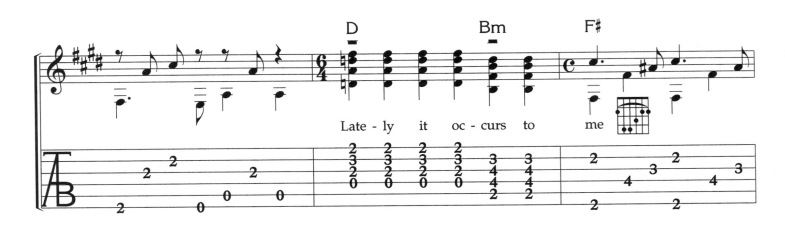

Late-ly it oc-curs to me

what a long, strange trip it's been.

SOLO

50

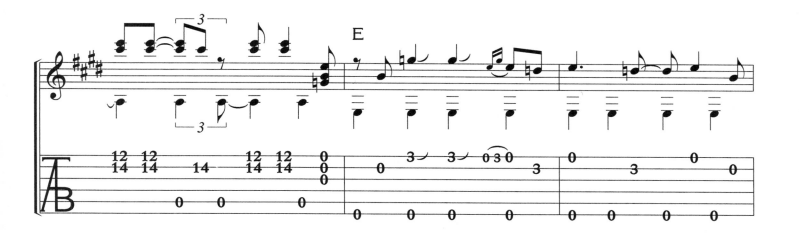

ENDING   *ritard.*

Truckin'
Lead Sheet

by Garcia, Hunter, Weir & Lesh   Copyright © 1971 Ice Nine Publishing Company, Inc.

1. Truckin', got my chips cashed in, keep truckin' like the doo dah man.
   Together, more or less in line, just keep truckin' on.

   Arrows of neon and flashing marquees out on Main Street,
   Chicago, New York, Detroit, it's all the same street.
   The typical city involved in the typical daydream.
   Hang it up and see what tomorrow brings.

2. Dallas got a soft machine. Houston, too close to New Orleans.
   New York got the ways and means but just won't let you be.

   Most of the cats that you meet on the street speak of true love.
   Most of the time they're sittin' and cryin' at home.
   One of these days they know they gotta get goin'.
   Out of the door and into the street all alone.

3. Truckin', like the doo dah man once told me, "You got to play your hand.
   Sometimes the cards ain't worth a dime if you don't lay 'em down."

   Bridge:
   Sometimes the light's all shinin' on me, other times I can barely see.
   Lately it occurs to me what a long, strange trip it's been.

4. What in the world ever became of sweet Jane?
   She lost her sparkle, you know she isn't the same.
   Livin' on reds, vitamin C and cocaine.
   All her friends can say is, "Ain't it a shame."

5. Truckin' up to Buffalo, been thinkin', you got to mellow slow.
   Takes time, too, you pick a place to go, just keep truckin' on.

   Sittin' and starin' out of the hotel window,
   Got a tip they're gonna kick the door in again.
   I like to get some sleep before I travel,
   But if you got a warrant, I guess you're gonna come in.

6. Busted, down on Bourbon Street, set up like a bowling pin,
   Knocked down, it gets to wearin' thin. They just won't let you be.

   You're sick of hangin' around and you'd like to travel.
   Get tired of travelin', you wanna settle down.
   I guess they can't revoke your soul for trying.
   Get out of the door, light out and look all around   *(bridge)*

7. Truckin', I'm a-goin' home. Oh baby, that's where I belong.
   Back home, sit down and patch my bones and get back truckin' on.

Video Lessons by Fred Sokolow

The Music Of Paul Simon
Arranged for
Fingerstyle Guitar
Taught by Fred Sokolow
* * * * * * * * * * * * * * * * * * * *
90-min video • Level 2
80 page tab/music booklet
GW 501 $29.95
* * * * * * * * * * * * * * * * * * * *
featuring The Boxer, Scarborough Fair,
American Tune, Bridge Over Troubled
Water, Mrs. Robinson, Hearts and Bones,
Me and Julio Down By The Schoolyard,
59th Street Bridge Song (Feelin' Groovy)
and Mother and Child Reunion

The Music Of Bob Dylan
Arranged for
Fingerstyle Guitar
Taught by Fred Sokolow
* * * * * * * * * * * * * * * * * * * *
90-min video • Level 2
72 page tab/music booklet
GW 502 $29.95
* * * * * * * * * * * * * * * * * * * *
featuring Lay Lady Lay, My Back Pages,
I Shall Be Released, Blowin' In The Wind,
Don't Think Twice, Mr. Tambourine Man,
Just Like Tom Thumb's Blues,
Too Much Of Nothing and
The Times They Are A Changing

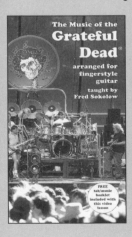

The Music of the
Grateful Dead
Taught by
Fred Sokolow
* * * * * * * * * * * * * * * * * * * *
92-min video • Level 2
80 page tab/music booklet
GW 503 $29.95
* * * * * * * * * * * * * * * * * * * *
featuring Friend of the Devil,
Ripple, Sugar Magnolia,
Touch Of Grey,
Uncle John's Band, Truckin',
Alabama Getaway,
Dire Wolf and Deal

Learn how to play and sing classic Paul Simon, Bob Dylan and Grateful Dead tunes from start to finish. Each of these video lessons will teach you how to fingerpick backup arrangements while singing, how to play instrumental solos and how to begin and end each song. While studying Fred Sokolow's arrangements you will also learn a lot about fingerpicking: backup patterns, soloing ideas and various chord positions.

Each song is played at regular speed and then slowed down with a split-screen that gives you a close-up look at the picking as well as chording hand. All the arrangements are clearly written out in tab and music in the accompanying booklet along with lead sheets and lyrics.

Beginner's
Blues Guitar
Taught by
Fred Sokolow
* * * * * * * * * * * * * * * * * * * *
70-min video • Level 1
48 page tab/music booklet
GW 401 $29.95
* * * * * * * * * * * * * * * * * * * *

In this video lesson, Fred Sokolow starts at the very beginning: tuning up and playing simple chords but by the end of this lesson you will be playing the blues in several keys, strumming and fingerpicking.

You'll know how to play:
• *Blues turnarounds.*
• *Boogie Woogie bass lines.*
• *Several strumming and fingerpicking patterns.*
• *Blues solos, licks and accompaniment styles of Lightnin' Hopkins, Big Bill Broonzy, Jimmy Reed, Mississippi John Hurt and others.*
• *Classic blues tunes like How Long Blues, Keys To The Highway, Baby What You Want Me To Do, Blues With a Feeling and Hesitation Blues.*

Playing &
Understanding
Jazz Guitar
Taught by
Fred Sokolow
* * * * * * * * * * * * * * * * * * * *
75-min video • Level 2/3
40 page tab/music booklet
GW 406 $29.95
* * * * * * * * * * * * * * * * * * * *

Jazz is one of the most challenging and satisfying styles of music you can play on the guitar. This video lesson presents a very clear and thorough introduction to jazz guitar. You will study all the licks, chords, scales and theory that you will need to know to get started. In this 75 minute lesson Fred Sokolow shows you:
• *Chord construction and chord types, including inversions and diminished chords.*
• *Scalewise progressions and how to use them.*
• *Circle-of-fifths progressions and how to play and recognize them.*
• *Chord comping, chord soloing and playing single-note solos to standards like I Got Rhythm, Honeysuckle Rose and Watch What Happens.*
• *How to improvise solos using scales and chord-based licks.*
• *How to solo over II-V-I standard changes.*

Bottleneck Slide Guitar
Acoustic & Electric Guitar Techniques
Taught by Fred Sokolow

* *

73-min video • Level 1/2
56 page tab/music booklet
GW 409 $29.95

* *

Nothing sounds as bluesy as a slide guitar, and this 70 minute video shows you how it's done on electric and acoustic, solo or with a group. Using classic blues tunes – *Little Red Rooster, Sittin' On Top Of The World, Reconsider Baby, The Sky Is Crying, Farther On Up The Road* and *One Way Out* – Fred Sokolow shows you how to play and improvise slide in the styles of the great bluesmen – Muddy Waters, Elmore James, Mississippi Fred McDowell and Duane Allman.

In this video lesson you will learn:
- *Solos, backup licks, turnarounds and fills in three tunings: open G, open D and standard.*
- *How to play slide in any key.*
- *How to improvise solos in standard and open tunings using moveable blues boxes.*

This video is a great introduction to the soulful world of bottleneck/slide guitar.

Rockabilly Guitar
Taught by Fred Sokolow

* *

73-min video • Level 2
48 page tab/music booklet
GW 403 $29.95

* *

Rockabilly is the roots of rock. It combines electric blues, country blues, Merle Travis-style fingerpicking and more. Using classic rockabilly tunes like *Blue Suede Shoes, Little Sister, That's All Right Mama, Matchbox Blues* and *That'll Be The Day,* Fred Sokolow shows the styles and techniques needed to play rockabilly guitar solos and backup. By the end of this hour-plus session, you'll know how to play:
- *Boogie Woogie backup licks.*
- *Turnarounds.*
- *Classic key of E blues/rock licks.*
- *Moveable blues/rock scales*
- *Fingerpicking patterns.*
- *Licks and solos of Buddy Holly, Carl Perkins, Eddie Cochran, Scotty Moore and Chuck Berry.*

Electric Blues Guitar
Taught by Fred Sokolow

* *

80-min video • Level 2
48 page tab/music booklet
GW 404 $29.95

* *

If you want to play blues guitar like B.B. King, Eric Clapton or Buddy Guy then this 80 minute video will get you on track. You'll learn:
- *Several moveable scale patterns for soloing.*
- *Moveable chords for backup.*
- *How to play melodies, chord backup and improvised solos on blues classics Stormy Monday, Everyday I Have The Blues, Killing Floor and Baby Please Don't Go.*
- *Intros and endings.*
- *Enough theory to understand the 12-bar blues structure and be able to play backup and solo in any key.*
- *Boogie bass lines, vibrato, note-bending and more.*

Beginner's Country Guitar
Taught by Fred Sokolow

* *

65-min video • Level 1/2
40 page tab/music booklet
GW 407 $29.95

* *

Country music is more popular than ever and all you need to put over a good country song is your voice and a guitar. This video gives you the tools you need to play old-fashioned country, honky-tonk and country rock. Playing classics like *Blue Eyes Crying In The Rain, I'm So Lonesome I Could Cry, The Bottle Let Me Down, I'm Movin' On, Will The Circle Be Unbroken, Silver Wings* and *Jambalaya,* Fred Sokolow shows you the basics of country guitar. You'll learn how to play: *Accompaniment strums for different rhythmic feels • A variety of first-position chords • Bass runs • Major scales • Solos and turnarounds*

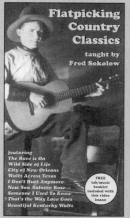

Flatpicking Country Classics
Taught by Fred Sokolow

* *

92-min video • Level 1/2
64 page tab/music booklet
GW 410 $29.95

* *

All you need to put over a good country song is your voice and a guitar. In this video Fred teaches nine standards every country picker/singer should know... from start to finish. You'll learn an intro for each song, a backup pattern and bass runs to play while singing, an instrumental solo, and an ending.

Picking up where his **BEGINNER'S COUNTRY GUITAR** video left off, Fred keeps the arrangements fairly simple but includes a few up-the-neck chord positions and hot licks. You'll learn solos and runs in five different keys. Each song is played at regular speed and then slowed down on a split-screen that gives you a close-up look at the picking hand and the chording hand. All the arrangements are clearly written out in tab and music in the accompanying booklet, along with lyrics.

Titles include: New San Antonio Rose, Wild Side of Life, Waltz Across Texas, The Race is On, Beautiful Kentucky Waltz, That's the Way Love Goes, I Don't Hurt Any more, Someone I Used To Know and *City of New Orleans*

CD Track Listings

This book comes with two compact discs. These CDs are the audio tracks from the video lesson of the same name. You can obtain detailed information about Fred's various video lessons from Stefan Grossman's Guitar Workshop, PO Box 802, Sparta, NJ 07871 or by visiting our website www.guitarvideos.com. Below is a detailed listing of how we have divided the tracks on these CDs:

CD Lesson One

Track 1: Musical intro
Track 2: Spoken introduction
Track 3: Performance of *Friend of the Devil*
Track 4: Tuning
Track 5: Teaching of *Friend of the Devil*
Track 6: Playing slowly *Friend of the Devil*
Track 7: Intro to *Deal*
Track 8: Performance of *Deal*
Track 9: Teaching of *Deal*
Track 10: Playing slowly *Deal*
Track 11: Intro to *Ripple*
Track 12: Performance of *Ripple*
Track 13: Teaching of *Ripple*
Track 14: Playing slowly *Ripple*
Track 15: Intro to *Alabama Getaway*
Track 16: Performance of *Alabama Getaway*
Track 17: *Teaching of Alabama Getaway*
Track 18: Playing slowly *Alabama Getaway*
Track 19: Intro to *Dire Wolf*
Track 20: Performance of *Dire Wolf*
Track 21: Teaching of *Dire Wolf*
Track 22: Playing slowly *Dire Wolf*

CD Lesson Two

Track 1: Intro to *Uncle John's Band*
Track 2: Performance of *Uncle John's Band*
Track 3: Teaching of *Uncle John's Band*
Track 4: Playing slowly *Uncle John's Band*
Track 5: More teaching of *Uncle John's Band*
Track 6: Intro to *Touch of Grey*
Track 7: Performance of *Touch of Grey*
Track 8: Teaching of *Touch of Grey*
Track 9: Playing slowly *Touch of Grey*
Track 10: Intro to *Sugar Magnolia*
Track 11: Performance of *Sugar Magnolia*
Track 12: Teaching of *Sugar Magnolia*
Track 13: Playing slowly *Sugar Magnolia*
Track 14: Intro to *Truckin'*
Track 15: Performance of *Truckin'*
Track 16: Tuning for *Truckin'*
Track 17: Teaching of *Truckin'*
Track 18: Playing slowly *Truckin'*
Track 19: Closing thoughts
Track 20: Closing music